From Ordinary to Extraordinary Using Dr. Tekemia Dorsey's (DTD) Transformational Leadership Models

360 Degrees of Evolution

Dr. Tekemia Dorsey

From Ordinary to Extraordinary

Additional Books and Media
by Dr. Tekemia Dorsey
can be purchased at
www.drtekemiadorsey.org (Personal Brand)
www.thecreativegrp.org (Company Website)

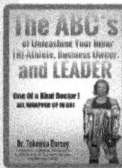

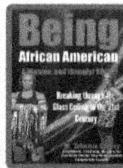

TABLE OF CONTENTS

Dr. Tekemia Dorsey's (DTD) Transformational Leadership Models

DEDICATION

This book is dedicated to my kids, Brandon "Bran", Heaven "Princess", Halee "Comet" and Beloved Joshua "BJ." They are my rock and the reason why I keep fighting to make a difference. I just hope and pray that the difference is made and acknowledged before God calls me home. #MyLegacyLivesThroughThem

I do what I do and I am who I am to leave a legacy for them and in them, they will be proud to say, "My Mom did that!"

Dr. Tekemia Dorsey's (DTD) Transformational Leadership Models

ACKNOWLEDGEMENTS

My Heavenly Father

Thank you God for the ongoing push in life, for removing from my life things that provided comfort and distraction. Comfort and distraction kept me in a box, leading me nowhere fast. Being in a comfort zone and distracted kept me from allowing the knowledge and wisdom you have bestowed upon me to be shared with the world, therefore not giving you all the glory deserved, not allowing me to reach those people needing the assistance required for their own success. I apologize publicly for being disobedient and ask for "forgiveness" for I am not worthy of this 55th chance again you are providing. After 8 years of nudging and countless people and signs sent my way, here it is. Here it is, a tool that will make a difference in others' lives taking them from *ordinary people to extraordinary leaders* in their own right. You are MAGNIFICENT to me!

The University of Phoenix and New Psalmist Baptist Church

I would like to thank my alma mater, the University of Phoenix who propelled my thought process and who stretched me beyond my limits as a doctoral candidate and now as a doctoral holder. From my teammate, Dr. William "Stan" Boddie who partnered with me from the beginning of my doctoral journey to the very end, thank you. We were the only 2nd "two person team" in UOP's history (at the time) to begin and end the doctoral process together (successfully and on time); to my

Dr. Tekemia Dorsey's (DTD) Transformational Leadership Models fellow cohort members; my dissertation chair, Dr. Freda Turner and committee members who also successfully contributed to my journey as a person, a doctoral holder, a leader in my field, and a pillar in my community, a hearty thank you as well.

Each component of my doctoral journey helped me to become the person I am and to help propel me to do the wonderful things beyond my doctoral process that I have achieved and things yet to be completed. I owe a debt of gratitude to the research participants that took part in my research study as well as my church, New Psalmist Baptist Church and its Discipleship Ministry Program because knowledge and wisdom acquired as a student and applied in my life led me to create my transformational leadership models (one secular and one spiritual).

Private Schools & Students

I would like to thank Baltimore White Marsh Seventh Day Adventist and Life Source Christian School (formerly Kingdom Academy) administration, staff, and students that allowed me for six years to teach my leadership development and training program in their institutions of higher learning, voluntarily. I literally set out to see if leadership development and training could be taught on the primary level and so I was given an opportunity to pilot my program for the first year and subsequent years to follow. This opportunity helped me to review, refine, and readjust my curriculum based off the feedback from K-12 students, parents and staff with support from administrators. From this feedback, my spiritual leadership model was mimic into a secular one, when I witnessed the true value it possessed and the impact it would have *transforming ordinary people into extraordinary leaders.*

There were many highlights during my time voluntarily teaching these students leadership development and training that would forever change their views and behaviors in life but none more important than being blessed in teaching my first born son, Brandon C. Johnson from 2nd grade to 8th grade leadership training that has helped to shape and mold his life and outlook on the world and later on, my oldest daughter, Heaven Simons as well. As a mother, I could not have asked for more.

While setting out to teach my leadership development and training curriculum and program to students, I in fact was taught myself and became the student. These students taught me exactly what I knew to be true, if taught early enough in life leadership development and training, it will show up through action and behavior when the time is right for them. They in turn taught me that *"True Leadership Lies In the POWER of the HOLY SPIRIT!"*™ *Dr. Tekemia Dorsey*

To all of my 500 plus students in K-12 in these two organizations over the six year span I was with you and that completed the program with Certificate of Completion for Leadership Development and Training from me, a resounding "THANK YOU" from the bottom of my heart. It was well worth it and I would not change a thing because

Dr. Tekemia Dorsey's (DTD) Transformational Leadership Models my payment was simply witnessing the growth and development that transpired in each and every one of you over the years.

Marvin J. Perry

About 6 or 7 years ago, I got a call from a gentlemen who I had begun to work with on several projects but without success in the end, who knew my value right away and had encouraged me to take the concepts of my models, curriculum, programs, youth leadership books, and education books and to place them into one centralized location, yet another book. I heard but ignored because I did not want to write yet another book. Little did I know this book would the very catalyst I needed on so many personal and professional levels to execute what I have always wanted to do; *help transform ordinary people into ordinary leaders.*

In his eyes, this book would solidify me as the *EXPERT* in my field that I had already been for years and so that other experts would learn of me, my transformational leadership models' importance and impact without having to go through my other books and media. What has held up success in our joint ventures was that of this tool; a tool I fought long and hard not to complete until being pushed more here in 2015 by God. Lessons on wisdom and obedience….. Well that is another book. ☺ God continue to work in mysterious ways.

Marvin J. Perry of PCG & Associates thanks for the push and acknowledgement years ago of what you knew was needed. I look forward now to allowing those unsuccessful projects we begin to reach their full potential in the years to come, God willing. If not, thanks so much for the time shared and knowledge transmitted along the way.

The BizTruth

Huge shout out to Carolyn Herfuth, my business coach for providing topics to come at a time for exploration to unveil in me what had been buried for a while, to force a propelled forward action inward for success, and also simply caring about me, more than what money would ever put a price on. I am blessed to call you my *FRIEND*.

I would like to thank "Lee Murphy-Wolf" my fellow Mighty Sister in Carolyn Herfuth's Evolve Accelerator 9 Cohort during one of our joint collaborative calls where our challenge was to discuss our "I Believes" and "Core Pillars" of our business and after I shared my topics, she said, "Tekemia, what came to mind while you were talking was the term '360 Degrees of Evolution.'"

Lee's comments reminded me of why I developed these models 10 years ago and "the term" that I allowed to escape me after a while from not promoting it. So thanks Lee for reminding me of that, I appreciate you, Fellow Mighty! Thanks Carolyn for bringing us together for this collaborative teamwork assignment.

Organizations Who Said "No"

Over the last six years, I have been trying to get a job, with organizations for positions that truly may not have inspired me but I thought I would be a good fit and they say repeatedly said, "NO!" I struggled with understanding doors were constantly

Dr. Tekemia Dorsey's (DTD) Transformational Leadership Models shut. It was simply because there was a greater purpose needing fulfillment, so a hearty thank you as well. The world cannot deny what has spiritually been ordained. I appreciate those doors being closed, so this one could be opened.

ABOUT THE AUTHOR

Dr. Tekemia Dorsey, CEO of The Creative GRP, LLC and Founder of Dr. Tekemia Dorsey's (DTD) Institute 2 Transform Leaders. She has a Doctorate of Management in Organizational Leadership from the University of Phoenix. Dr. Dorsey founded her Institute 2 Transform Leaders in 2005 during her last semester in her doctoral program. Dr. Dorsey was unsure at that time, the enormous impact her leadership development and training models/programs would have on youth to adults.

Using the leadership principles and core pillars from her Institute 2 Transform Leaders, Dr. Dorsey went on to become an established and awarding winner author, business owner, and athlete. She is a keynote speaker, facilitator/workshop presenter, curriculum specialist, publisher, professor, entrepreneur, radio show host, executive leadership trainer/coach, community activist, athlete and a Child of God. Dr. Dorsey currently serves in a voluntarily capacity as Commissioner of Baltimore City Parks and Recreations Co-Ed Christian Softball League and as President/Executive Director for The International Association of Black Triathletes.

Dr. Dorsey is a Marathoner, Triathlete, Duathlete, and an IRONMAN! She is a member of Zeta Phi Beta Sorority, Inc.; was named ALIVE MAGAZINE's 2011 "Woman of the Year" & a Finalist for Doreen Rainey's 2011 "Radical Woman of the Year" Award; was

Dr. Tekemia Dorsey's (DTD) Transformational Leadership Models named one of The National Association of Women on the Rise 2011 "10 Most Intriguing Women and received a Woman of POWER Award in January, 2011. Dr. Tekemia Dorsey has received numerous awards and honors but remains most proud of the Proclamations given by Governor Martin O'Malley and Mayor Stephanie Rawlings-Blake in honor of the work done on behalf of youth, parents, and the community in her city/state in 2011.

Dr. Tekemia Dorsey's (DTD) Institute 2 Transform Leaders

Dr. Dorsey envisioned her institute making positive contributions in the field of leadership as well as assisting millions of ordinary people transforming into extraordinary leaders. She will be launching her online programs by mid-May 2015 as well as continuing to teach grounded courses using her leadership principles and core pillars.

Dr. Tekemia Dorsey's
Institute 2 Transform Leaders

Learn more at www.drtekemiadorsey.org or www.thecreativegrp.org

DESCRIPTION OF THE BOOK

This book provides a brief synopsis into both of Dr. Tekemia Dorsey's (DTD) Transformational Leadership Models (Secular VS Spiritual) that were created in 2006 but were originally leadership development, training and education models (Secular and Spiritual). Dr. Tekemia Dorsey's Transformational Leadership Models evolved from extensive research and semi-structure and structure interviews with over 100 educators, leaders, supervisors, parents and teachers from 2004 – 2007.

DTD's Transformational Leadership Models were originally Leadership Development Training and Education Models that were piloted to elementary and middle school aged youth in Private Christian school settings from 2007 – 2010. In 2010, the secular leadership development, training and education model/curriculum was adopted by a public school system in Baltimore City that served at-risk youth. The curriculum was enhanced from its previous version to meet the needs of young adults' ages 16 to 21 years.

Once the population expanded to a new targeted audience served (business owners, entrepreneurs, corporations, workforce development centers, etc), DTD's Transformational Leadership Model dropped its education component to focus more on the core pillars of the transformational leadership models.

Dr. Tekemia Dorsey's (DTD) Transformational Leadership Models
Dr. Tekemia Dorsey's (DTD) Transformational Leadership Models are designed to take ordinary people and transform them to extraordinary leaders through 360 degrees of evolution through a focus on nine core pillars.

PREFACE

I wrote this book to share with the world these amazing transformational leadership models developed from research, theory, interviews, it encompass core pillars that add value to the person and to leadership positions, organizations, relationships, families, society and what's most important, self.

Growing up in the inner city of Baltimore, being raised by my grandmother, and was labeled as a juvenile delinquent, expected to barefoot and pregnant before 16 and was told by my high school guidance counselor that I was only worthy of working at McDonald's and that even applying for a trade/technical school and definitely, a four-year college/university is out of my reach.

Despite the thoughts of those individuals that includes educators and family members, I had people around me that believed enough in me, they encouraged and motivated me and in time, I began to believe in myself. In college, I had additional women in leadership positions that believed in me as well and so I wanted to be like them.

When I traveled through my doctoral studies, I begin to understand that people who lead effectively are not those that possess a certain position but in fact certain qualities about self.

I used my time as a doctoral candidate to research, interview, learn, develop and refine my topic of interest, which remains leadership

Dr. Tekemia Dorsey's (DTD) Transformational Leadership Models development and training. This process assisted in the birth of these two leadership models.

I possess a Doctorate of Management in Organizational Leadership and have owned and operated a small business consulting and training firm since 2006. I serve as Executive Director of International Association of Black Triathletes and Commissioner of Co-Ed Christian Softball League. I have served on multiple panels and in other various leadership roles and positions over a 20-year time span.

I have used the core values in my leadership models to become an Ironman, a marathoner, a triathlete, and a duathlete. To become a leader in my community and to lead others through programs, positions held and to develop relationships with others.

As an expert in Leadership Development and Training, here are my beliefs and core pillars on which my training, programs, products and services are based on.

I believe

I believe foundational principles of a person (ethics, morals, values, character) help him/her to better answer the question WHO AM I;

I believe that process outweighs the outcome so CRITICAL THINKING through decisions are key to success, that there is no "I" in team, so TEAM BUIDING is a necessary component to great leadership; and that understanding, acknowledging and embracing the CULTURAL DIVERSITY that encompass the world will take people far in leadership roles and positions;

I believe that leaders should be more transformational then transactional in nature and in application and in order to accomplish that, you must understand what motivates you, is it REAL WORLD EVENTS or SPIRITUAL GUIDANCE?;

I believe youth are the catalyst for change leadership in the future and once any individual recognize their LEADERSHIP ATTRIBUTES, he/she will begin to lead by example;

I believe that COMMUNICATION can make or break relationships and the more people understand how to communicate effectively, the more relationships can flourish and develop;

I believe people transform their environments and cultures by BEING TRANSFORMATIONAL in their actions, behaviors, and words;

I believe that for 360 Degrees of Evolution to happen, people need to be consistent in their actions, be honest with self, and be willing to explore WHO AM I daily....

Dr. Tekemia Dorsey

Dr. Tekemia Dorsey's (DTD) Transformational Leadership Models

INTRODUCTION

This book discuss the core pillars of Dr. Tekemia Dorsey's Transformational Leadership Models. Each pillar is discussed individually and how they work collectively supporting one another. When applied successfully an individual will truly experience *360 Degrees of Evolution* that allows **ordinary people to become extraordinary leaders**. While each pillar is followed as a continuous spectrum of development by following the suggested pattern (featured below), individuals experience the 360 Degrees of Evolution mentioned above, however the pillars can be harnessed individually and still remain just as powerful when mastered.

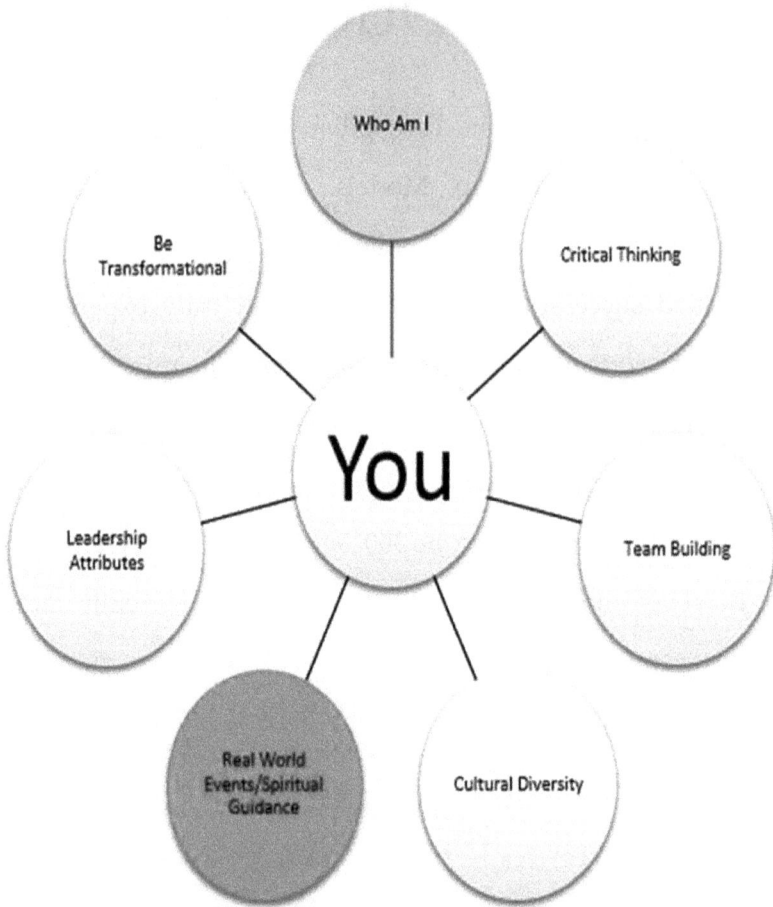

Dr. Tekemia Dorsey's (DTD)

Transformational Leadership Models

360 Degrees of Evolution

Dr. Tekemia Dorsey's (DTD) Transformational Leadership Models

The core pillars of DTD's Transformational Leadership Model are discussed in this book individually. Each one is an independent pillar of its own but are also dependent on one another for success as a leader. Through stories and real life scenarios, the model itself are shared in practical application in how they work together to have ordinary people transformed into extraordinary leaders by experiencing the *360 Degrees of Evolution.*

The DTD's Transformational Leadership Models are universal across industries and disciplines respectively and is applicable to individuals from individuals such as youth, to CEO's of Corporation.

This book should be used interchangeably in academic settings and business cultures and environments. The contents of this book can be used as part of curriculum for youth in primary grades and on secondary levels, for those individuals going through workforce development programs, for students who are pursuing advanced degrees, for individuals looking to start a business, enhance their business, or to climb that ladder of success in positions within their corporate settings.

The DTD's Transformational Leadership Models core pillars are ones that focus on personal growth and development of a person and their behaviors. The content of the book can be used as part of any structural program, training or activity that focuses on improvement of

Dr. Tekemia Dorsey's (DTD) Transformational Leadership Models self, soft skills development and as such but not limited to professional development, leadership training, personal growth and development.

Definition of Terms

- **Who Am I** – finding out and exploring one's purpose and passion in life.

- **Critical Thinking** - disciplined **thinking** that is clear, rational, open-minded, and informed by evidence.

- **Team Building** - the use of different types of **team** interventions that are aimed at enhancing social relations and clarifying **team** members' roles as well as solving task and interpersonal problems that affect team functioning.

- **Cultural Diversity** - is the acceptance of the various ethnic cultures in schools, organizations, businesses, neighborhoods or cities. At the best, it involves treating impartially and fairly each ethnic group without promoting the particular beliefs or values of any group.

- **Real World Events** – events of the world that occur daily in and around society.

- **Leadership Attributes** – defined as characteristics, behaviors, and actions of the individual that help in the identification of the person.

- **Communication** – is defined as ways or processes of expressing feelings or ideas which can be through verbal and nonverbal mean, expressions, body language, and so forth.

- **Be Transformational** – the manner in which a person carries him/herself in the company of another, allowing their presence to impact positively on the environment or setting.

COMPELLING TRUTH

Personal

Growing up in the inner city streets of West Side Baltimore, it was in absence of my mother and father. I was raised by my grandmother in a very closely knit extended family. My aunts and uncles were more like brother and sisters and so were the large array of cousins that stayed or visited my grandmother's house. My identity was framed based on my surroundings, such as culture, environment, family beliefs, role models and there a lack of all of the above. My foundational principles include morals, values, and ethics.

The Streets

I learned values, morals, and ethics from my family but I gained common sense and smart decision making from the streets. Growing up on Lexington Street with my mother's side of the family living in the 2300 block West Lexington Street and my father's side of the family living in the 1800 block of West Lexington Street, I felt like I had the best of both worlds but in actuality I did not.

Family

I had the support of my family but not as much as I would have liked to but I valued it for what it was and what was needed to simply get ahead and get by in life. I learned early on those relationships in life that mattered most to me but I did not know how to cultivate those relationships.

Business

In business, I have learned by trial and error and now I have an opportunity to share in life, what was not shared with me in a way that is easy to follow, understand, and apply daily.

Dr. Tekemia Dorsey

Conceptual Component Summaries

1. *Who Am I?*—The key to being an effective leader is to have a true understanding of who you are as an individual and the roles that you play in your life circles. Participants begin to make the connections between their individual identities and the roles they play in their lives.

2. *Critical Thinking*—In order to develop a true understanding and application of the key components and characteristics of transformational leadership, participants explore the ways that they process and learn information in a variety of situations to develop a fundamental understanding of the ways in which they process information to make decisions as transformational leaders. Through an examination of Gardner's theory of Multiple Intelligences and Johari's Windows, participants have the opportunity to create their own strategic learning plan as the precursor to developing strategic plans for groups/teams that they may be leading through their roles as transformational leaders.

3. *Team Building*—A hallmark of transformational leaders is their ability to bring together individuals within a group to work together, collaborate effectively and ultimately grow into becoming leaders themselves—taking direct responsibility for the outcomes of their actions. Participants examine the dynamics of group interaction and the importance of team building in the transformational leadership process.

4. *Cultural Diversity*—A good transformational leader must consider the backgrounds and cultural footprints of their team in order to make sound decisions. As part of the unit, participants explore the effect that cultural norms, beliefs and ways of thinking affect group dynamics and impact leadership decisions across a variety of situations.

5. *Real World Events*—Participants examine real world events and critically assess the role of leaders in each situation. This examination of real-world application of leadership theory allows participants to further develop their understanding of the concepts presented.

6. *Leadership Attributes*—Participants examine the actions of leaders and have an opportunity to speak to community leaders to further develop their concept of the characteristics and roles of transformational leaders.

7. *Communication*—Participants examine the various ways in which messages are communicated—both verbal and nonverbal, and assesses their ability to communicate and interact effectively with various groups. The importance and role of communication in leadership is explored and participants have the opportunity to develop their own theories and strategies to improve communication within a group.

8. *Being Transformational*—This component provides participants with a way of putting the theory of Johari's Windows into practice

Dr. Tekemia Dorsey's (DTD) Transformational Leadership Models and identify various ways in which they can be transformational leaders in their communities.

9. *Who Am I*—This component provides participants with an opportunity to express who they are as transformational leaders, after have gone through each of the core pillars through this transformational leadership model.

You can surmise from the conceptual summaries of the core pillars, numbers 1 & 9 are both the same and that is not by mistake but rather by divine intervention.

Individuals begin the process of transformational leadership but exits the process as a new creature of habit and having experience 360 Degrees of Evolution. The 360 Degrees of Evolution occurs, when and only when, the individual is honest with self by identifying his/her strengths, areas of weaknesses and remains optimistic to change from stage one of the leadership model.

The nine core pillars of these transformational leadership models are not meant to be a means to an end, but a stepping stone or a continuation of self-exploration with a focus of leadership that leads to positive change and outcomes in one's life. Any of the core pillars can be made interchangeable with others pillars, models or program to add a stronger value to the objective and goal at hand.

Now let's drive deeper into the nine core pillars chosen for these transformational leadership models and further understand why they are so significant in the development of you are a leader.

Dr. Tekemia Dorsey's (DTD)
Transformational Leadership Models
360 Degrees of Evolution

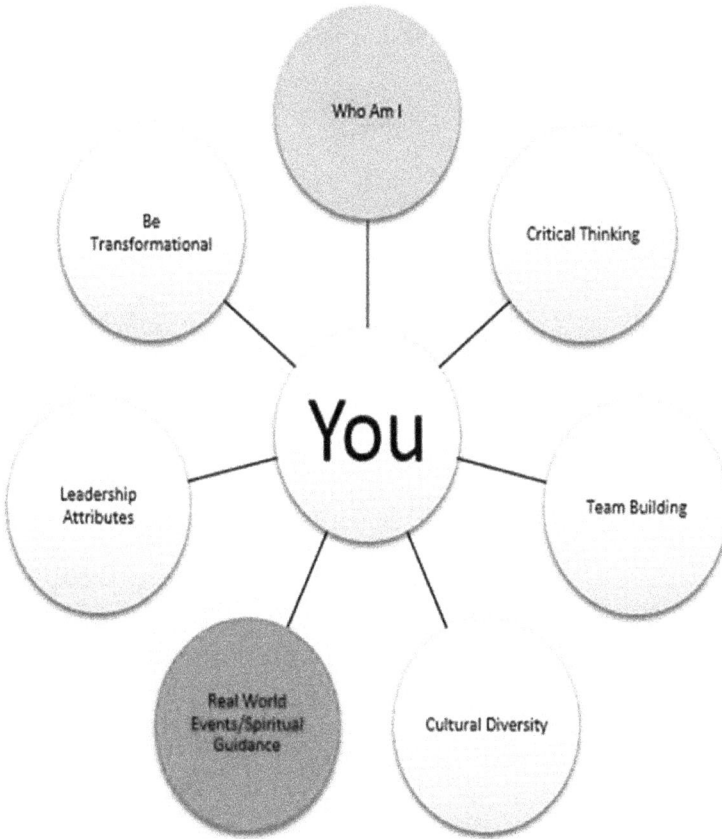

WHAT'S THE RELATIONSHIP BETWEEN DTD'S TRANSFORMATIONAL LEADERSHIP MODELS AND *LEADERSHIP DEVELOPMENT?*

Are leaders born or made? This discussion has been one that goes as far back as pre-historic dinosaurs, and depending on who you ask, can be answered one way or another. In my professional experience, leaders can be made and from my personal beliefs, leaders can be born.

From my personal beliefs, everyone is born with a soul; which is in essence connected to the Holy Spirit. Through the guidance and facilitation from the Holy Spirit, individuals learn to know what is right and what is wrong in life. Individuals learn to know what is right and what is wrong through their parents, environment, culture, surroundings, role models, and society.

Those that are trusted to lead and guide these individuals are also filled with the Holy Spirit. When individuals are connected and remain connected with the higher being he/she believes in and stay connected with that higher being, then transformation begins from the inside out versus the outside in, that remains evident in their behaviors, actions, communications, choices made and the way people are impacted (Positive versus Negative, Selfish gain versus Selfless gain, Transformational versus Transactional).

Dr. Tekemia Dorsey's (DTD) Transformational Leadership Models

Through the personal growth and development from a two-step process, leaders are born and not made. The two-step process encompasses the guidance and facilitation led by the Holy Spirit and executed by individuals. All that is really needed in life is that of belief and execution of what we really are and that is a spiritual being living in a borrowed body which is known as the "flesh" therefore the POWER we need to be Leaders already exist inside each and every one, It simply needs to be tapped into needs to simply be tapped into, but if it were that simple, I would not have developed DTD's Transformational Leadership Models or feel the need to write this book.

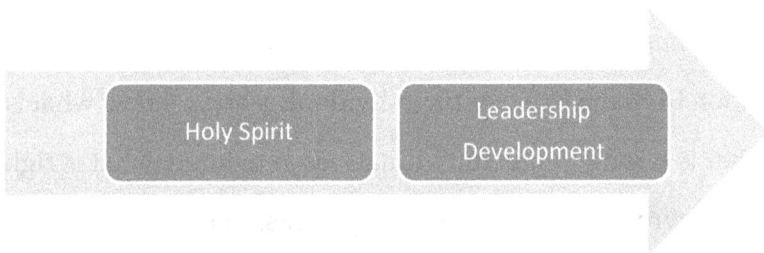

True Leadership Lies In the POWER of the HOLY SPIRIT

™ Dr. Tekemia Dorsey

From my professional experience, leaders can be made. Leaders are made through the quality of leadership development and training models and programs. Ones that can provide tangible outcomes and realistic tools for success. Leadership development models, training and programs that an individual can use and improve upon, not just those that are filled with fluff. Leadership development models, trainings, and programs that infuse research, theory, and practical application; one that has been validated and has a solid foundation that is applicable across one's growth and development stages; one or two such as Dr. Tekemia Dorsey's (DTD) Transformational Leadership Models.

Brief History – DTD's Transformational Leadership Models

Dr. Tekemia Dorsey's (DTD) Transformational Leadership Models (Secular VS Spiritual) which was created in 2006 but were originally leadership development, training and education models (Secular and Spiritual). Dr. Tekemia Dorsey's Transformational Leadership Models evolved from extensive research and semi-structure and structural interviews with over 100 educators, leaders, supervisors, parents and teachers from 2004 – 2007.

DTD's Transformational Leadership Models were originally Leadership Development Training and Education Models that were piloted to elementary and middle school aged youth in Private Christian school settings from 2007 – 2010. In 2010, the secular leadership development, training and education model/curriculum was adopted by a public school system in Baltimore City that served at-risk youth. The curriculum was enhanced from its previous version to meet the needs of young adults' ages 16 to 21 years young.

Dr. Tekemia Dorsey's (DTD) Transformational Leadership Models

Once the population expanded to a new targeted audience served (business owners, entrepreneurs, corporations, workforce development centers, etc), DTD's Transformational Leadership Model dropped its education component to focus more on the core pillars of the transformational leadership models.

Dr. Tekemia Dorsey's (DTD) Transformational Leadership Models are designed to take ordinary people and transform them to extraordinary leaders through 360 degrees of evolution through a focus on nine core pillars.

CORE **PILLAR** 1: *WHO AM I?*

It will take the span of one's life to truly understand the question WHO AM I? What makes this exciting is the fact that each day a person has breath, he/she has an opportunity to learn something new about "self" and to make a difference with that new found knowledge. On the contrary, what makes the exploration of self, less attractive is the facing of the untruth a person has held onto as a value and reality for so long. However, even the ugliest of ugly situations can be changed, if one truly wants change and transformation to occur.

The Struggle

It is a daily struggle for people to truly know, accept, and embrace who they are as an individual and in the multitude of roles they are involved in and their responsibilities on a daily basis. Women, who are in corporate positions, are wives, with children and other social responsibilities coupled with struggles they faced on a daily basis in their various communities.

Due to the nature of women to want to help and nurture others, they often overlook on many occasions their own needs and wants for that of others.

When women allow the needs of others to supersede their own, their worlds tends to be upside down. Instead of the woman being on top and

Dr. Tekemia Dorsey's (DTD) Transformational Leadership Models the world being her portal of endless opportunity for success, the world sits on the top and the woman at the bottom unsure of how to turn things around in her life

Picture 1.

Picture 2

a. Mental Struggle.

The #1 struggle for women, like all individuals whose world is turned upside down is that of their mental state. When a Woman's  mind is not at peace, not clear, not at ease and constantly racing then everything else in her life will be experiencing the same and it will affect decisions made, relationships engaged in, and negative behaviors such as fear, anxiety, procrastination, uncertainty, and low self-esteem continue to be a normal part of their daily behavior and routine. Poor decision making, unhealthy relationships, and the behaviors described above prohibit them from making positive attributes to them and everyone around them. If you ask a woman how she would break this cycle of trauma she is inflicting on herself and those directly and those around her, she would not be sure, but would want to believe her situation as not real.

b. Physical Struggle.

When a woman's state of mind is disconnected from her realities, another area of concern becomes their physical state. Women are emotional creatures and when they start to experience emotional or physical stress, they revert to food. The same goes true to cultural barriers that exist such as with African Americans and Hispanics, these cultures are known for their eating habits. These does not mean all African Americans and Hispanics are over eaters.

Some, maybe most women either eat their way through stress or workout stress related issues. Very few fall in the latter category but quite a few in the former category. When women experience fear, anxiety, uncertainty, procrastination, self-confidence, and even stress what is one of the most common behaviors exhibited to combat the disorder of their minds, their lives, and their situation? They eat. Things

Dr. Tekemia Dorsey's (DTD) Transformational Leadership Models such as chips, soda, candy, junk food, fried foods, massive sugar, and other unhealthy choices become the cure for the current problem which leads to an obese body and depression.

c. **Spiritual Struggle.**

Women are naturally spiritual creatures that believe in a power higher than self. World situations and the roles women take on such as a mother, wife, or even corporate executive are often time ones that do not allow too much time for self, unless it is on Sunday. Most women on Sundays simply want to rest and do nothing after a very busy week. Their spiritual connection which is balance for most women are then being sacrificed even more than usual.

When a woman's mental, physical and spiritual balances are not equal, then they will lack the peace of mind and a sense of self for success, often leaving them asking themselves, WHO AM I?

The question "WHO AM I" is an evolutionary concept that can take a lifetime to master however, the more one begins to examine who they are and what they stand for, how one handles the challenges of life makes all the difference. In the Dr. Tekemia Dorsey's (DTD) Transformational Leadership Model, many tools and assessments are used but one of my favorite remains that of Johari's Window.

The Johari window test was named after the first names of its inventors: Joseph Luft and Harry Ingham, *"Of Human Interaction"* (Mayfield Publishing Co., Palo Alto, CA: 1969).

The Johari window – which represents self – looks like this:

Before,

4

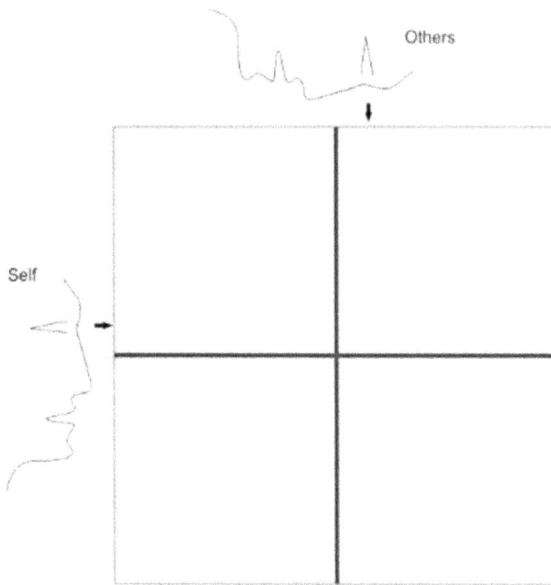

Others

Self

After,

Johari's Window is a tool used to help individuals become even more aware of self and to reaffirm self. This is a wonderful tool as a part of DTD's Transformational Leadership Model to assist people going from ordinary to extraordinary leaders.

I believe self-awareness is one of the greatest gifts we have in our tool box for success.

Dr. Tekemia Dorsey's (DTD) Transformational Leadership Models

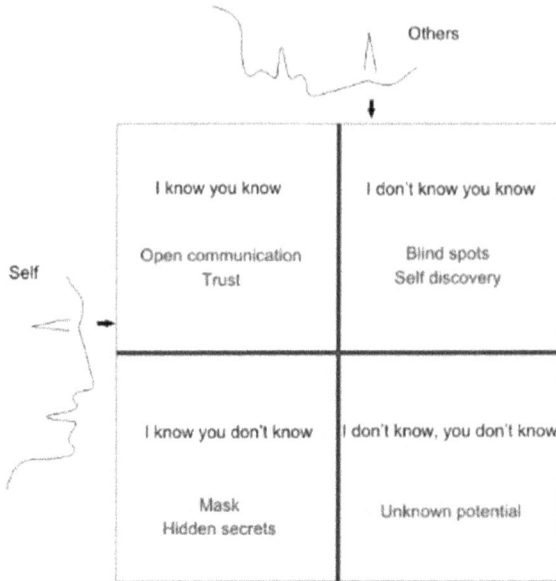

Others

I know you know Open communication Trust	I don't know you know Blind spots Self discovery
I know you don't know Mask Hidden secrets	I don't know, you don't know Unknown potential

Self

In the Dr. Tekemia Dorsey's (DTD) Transformational Leadership Model, the key to being an effective leader is to have a true understanding of who you are as an individual and the roles that you play in your life circles. Participants begin to make the connections between their individual identities and the roles they play in their lives during the exploration of the core pillar, WHO AM I?

CORE PILLAR 2: *CRITICAL THINKING*

Humans by nature keep their hands in more than their fair share of the cookie jar. When this happens, they are left overwhelmed, unsure, and scatter-brained to say the least. Instead of them being able to provide a roadmap to success for self, they tend to go into any direction that leaves them frustrated, upset, bewildered, anxious, and panicky.

Women who wear many hats such as wife, mother, community leader, community organizer, community volunteer, or even corporate executive has their fair share of days where everything and everyone one has a lot in common.

For a corporate executive, responsibilities such as administrative, decision making, personnel, meetings on various levels, trainings, conferences, workshops, and a few other things during the course of the day are just a few things needing attention.

Dr. Tekemia Dorsey's (DTD) Transformational Leadership Models

Then, if that corporate executive is a mom, she now has Mommy duties which requires attention just as those given at work including homework,

teacher conferences, follow ups, concerns and let's not consider if it is more than one child she has.

A woman's daily schedule with her family for the day could very much reflect the following:

Semi Aggressive Family Schedule

6:00 AM – Wake Up - Mommy

6:30 AM – Family Dress, Breakfast

7:00 AM – Drop off to Daycare/School

7:15 AM – Off to work

8:30 AM – Arrive to work

5:00 PM – Leave from work

6:30 PM – Pick up family from Aftercare

7:00 PM – Arrive Home

7:30 PM – Eat Dinner

8:00 PM – Check homework

9:30 PM – Prayer/Bedtime for Family

9:45 PM – Mommy off to bed

Now this potential scheduling which is very reflective of an average family with kids is truly aggressive but what is missing is the activity which most kids today are involved in.

Where in the course of the day does the mother have to herself; to think act or engage self or life? What impact can a schedule like this have on the mind, body, spirit, and soul after a while?

Now let's examine the same family dynamics with activities built in:

Aggressive Family Schedule

6:00 AM – Wake Up - Mommy

6:30 AM – Family Dress, Breakfast

7:00 AM – Drop off to Daycare/School

7:15 AM – Off to work

8:30 AM – Arrive to work

4:00 PM – Leave work early

5:30 PM – Pick up family from Aftercare

6:00 PM – Sports Activities (Practice/Games)

8:30 PM – Pick up dinner from fast food place

9:00 PM – Arrive Home

9:15 PM – Eat Dinner

9:45 PM – Check homework

10:45 PM - Bath

11:15 PM – Prayer/Bedtime for Family

12:00 AM – Mommy off to bed

This schedule in conjunction with the schedule above (Semi Aggressive Family Schedule) are realistic today for parents with active

Dr. Tekemia Dorsey's (DTD) Transformational Leadership Models kids. what happens is burn out, exhaustion, poor body image, unhealthy decision making, irritability, low self-esteem, lack of intimacy and most importantly, and a loss of self.

In the Dr. Tekemia Dorsey's (DTD) Transformational Leadership Models, a multitude of assessments and tools are used for success but one of my favorite is that of Howard Gardener's Multiple Intelligences. Through the use of this tool, one's talents are discovered and applied for success.

Below are Howard Gardner's Multiple Intelligences Theory and a simple grid diagram that illustrates his seven multiple intelligences model at a glance.

Howard Gardner's Multiple Intelligence Simple Grid

intelligence type	capability and perception
Linguistic	words and language
Mathematical	logic and numbers
Musical	music, sound, rhythm
Bodily-Kinesthetic	body movement control
Spatial-Visual	images and space
Interpersonal	other people's feelings
Intrapersonal	self-awareness

A mother with aggressive schedules such as above would learn their "intelligence language" drive deeper into its understanding and begin to make changes that allow a more balance sense of self however without learning about ones "intelligence language" and thinking critically through the situation presented, failure remains imminent.

In order to develop a true understanding and application of the key components and characteristics of transformational leadership, participants explore the various ways in which information is acquired in varieties of situations and ability to make decisions as transformational leaders. Through an examination of Gardner's theory of Multiple Intelligences and Johari's Windows, participants have the opportunity to create their own strategic learning plan as the precursor to developing strategic plans for real application in situations that they may be find themselves through their roles as transformational leaders, such as their families in this core pillar, *Critical Thinking*.

Dr. Tekemia Dorsey's (DTD) Transformational Leadership Models

CORE PILLAR 3: *TEAM BUILDING*

A woman with a family and active kids with Semi or Aggressive Family Schedules as discussed before and shared below, is displaying an "I" in a team because everything as it appears, is done by that one person. While the schedule provided, is one very reflective of families in America today, one or two elements could be added or removed but nevertheless, one person attempting to do it all is far from realistic.

Semi Aggressive Family Schedule

6:00 AM – Wake Up - Mommy

6:30 AM – Family Dress, Breakfast

7:00 AM – Drop off to Daycare/School

7:15 AM – Off to work

8:30 AM – Arrive to work

5:00 PM – Leave from work

6:30 PM – Pick up family from Aftercare

7:00 PM – Arrive Home

7:30 PM – Eat Dinner

8:00 PM – Check homework

9:30 PM – Prayer/Bedtime for Family

9:45 PM – Mommy off to bed

Dr. Tekemia Dorsey's (DTD) Transformational Leadership Models

With this semi aggressive family schedule, it is possible that one person could handle, has handled and will continue to handle it. However at what

costs? Is it at the expense of their sanity, mental state, physical appearance, energy level, relationships gained or lost, burn out and being overwhelmed?

Aggressive Family Schedule

6:00 AM – Wake Up - Mommy

6:30 AM – Family Dress, Breakfast

7:00 AM – Drop off to Daycare/School

7:15 AM – Off to work

8:30 AM – Arrive to work

4:00 PM – Leave work early

5:30 PM – Pick up family from Aftercare

6:00 PM – Sports Activities (Practice/Games)

8:30 PM – Pick up dinner from fast food place

9:00 PM – Arrive Home

9:15 PM – Eat Dinner

9:45 PM – Check homework

10:45 PM - Bath

11:15 PM – Prayer/Bedtime for Family

12:00 AM – Mommy off to bed

With this aggressive family schedule, it is possible that one person could handle it, has handled and will continue to handle it; however the likelihood of success over time is far greater than that of the semi aggressive family schedule. Here's why? The focus is more about the outcome than the process and leaves one to experience mental and physical breakdowns and at what costs? Is it that of their lack of sanity, mental state, physical appearance, energy level, relationships gained or lost, burn out and being overwhelmed, early death, aneurysms developed disassociation with reality?

It Takes a Village

The bible says it takes a village to raise a child; this metaphor can be adapted to any situation or scenario. In this case, it is one of a woman with a family and active kids that should not attempt to do things on her own that requires 24/7 care and implementation. In this situation what resources will this woman need to explore in term of opportunities; resources, and people who can assist her with one of more of the events in her schedule that will provide less of a wear and tear on her? How can she leverage to her support network to create a win-win scenario for her and her family. The key remains within self (no more, no less).

Women are individuals that believe they can do it all and can take on the world. Women believe that, depending on their cultural beliefs and family upbringing, they should try things themselves first and ask for help later.

Dr. Tekemia Dorsey's (DTD) Transformational Leadership Models

In essence there is nothing wrong with being responsible for what they desire to want out of life, but when does one realize when things become too much?

The benefits of openly communicating the need for help or assistance does not include one of being a loser or sell out. The benefits of seeking balance in life does not allude to the fact, one will be viewed as weak but in all honesty strong by those that matters most; the family and the kids.

There has been an emphasis during this pillar of teamwork on the individual mainly because while there is no "I" in team, before there is a team, a bunch of "I's" need to come to the table knowing his/her strengths and areas of challenges for an overall balance for success as part of a team and in the building of a team.

In this example, the more the woman know of herself (strengths and weaknesses) and things she need help with (an extra person for driving, support, etc), the more probable success factor in building a team will occur. On the contrary, if a woman in this scenario fails to identifies her strengths and weaknesses (who am I), think critically accessing her situation to determine success (critical thinking), and to begin to reach across parties lines for assistance (teamwork), she is destined to be less transformational in nature and more transactional, which benefits no one.

"A hallmark of transformational leaders is their ability to bring together individuals within a group to work together, collaborate effectively and

16

ultimately grow into becoming leaders themselves—taking direct responsibility for outcomes of their actions. Participants examine the dynamics of group interaction and the importance of team building in the transformational leadership process"

Dr. Tekemia Dorsey

Dr. Tekemia Dorsey's (DTD) Transformational Leadership Models

CORE PILLAR 4: *CULTURAL DIVERSITY*

The world is made up of diverse cultures but these concepts, individually and collectively are often not valued or identified as important. The world is made up of different people, with different backgrounds, similarities and differences but are not often accepted. This is a huge concern.

The similarities and differences in each of us is what makes us unique and odd but people are not really able to see, understand, and accept the differences of others. People say they do in theory but does not so much in application. Look at the scenarios regarding Michael Brown and Trayvon Martin, celebrities such as Kim Kardashian West and Kanye West, the public defamation and disrespect of our President, Barack Obama and First Lady Michelle Obama, just to name a few.

In the scenario with the active family woman, society would automatically place her in a category of "single and poor class" because a mate or husband has not been added to the script, how wrong could that assumption be? A person's bias and prejudice based on his/her upbringing, own culture and environment, foundational principles such as beliefs, morals, and values are those that add to the struggle of diversity in cultures or contribute positively to the charge because an individual is able to view another for who and what he/she is.

Dr. Tekemia Dorsey's (DTD) Transformational Leadership Models

The former is what happens 99.9% of the time, and the former less than .1%. The world is made up of a melting pot of cultures, races, ethnicities, various likes and dislikes, similarities and differences, beliefs, morals and values and each person is fearfully and wonderfully made in HIS (God's) image. It would be a powerful thing if we could respect one another for who and what we are, the world would be a better place. However in order for that to occur, the world would need to start all over again from scratch and be rid of the imperfection inherited over centuries that extend back to our ancestors.

When people are not able to value one another, then it makes it difficult for true partnerships and relationships to be formed. When a woman has experienced bad relationships, hurt, a lack of trust, pain, heartache and distress because of a person, especially one of statue or significance such as a leader, then that emotion or experience is now defined by that person. When a woman who needs assistance or seek help with a concern is forced to work with or settle for a person representative of a past mistake, then the outcome is not positive. As a result of that barrier, team work needed is not achieved. What will it take for a person to accept another person for what they represent?

In the Dr. Tekemia Dorsey's (DTD) Transformational Leadership Model, cultural diversity is thoroughly discussed, because understanding a person for who and what he/she is and represents is needed for short term and long term success. Most are not quick to trust another which bring a variety of concerns to the table (scenarios). The more educated a person is the more time he will take to explore others who are not well educated as he is through their ethnicity, culture, socioeconomic environment, religious affiliation, personal bias and prejudice, sexual orientation, political affiliation, and social cues.

"A good transformational leader must consider the backgrounds and cultural footprints of their team in order to make sound decisions. As a part of the unit, participants explore the effect of cultural norms, beliefs and ways of thinking affect group dynamics and impact leadership decisions across a variety of situations"

Dr. Tekemia Dorsey

CORE PILLAR 5:
Real World Events/Spiritual Guidance

People look at the world through different lens and the set of lens that appear the most real to them are those that their reality is based off. The two sets of lens referred here are *real world events* or *spiritual events.*

Real World Events

Most people are motivated by the events of the world. Those events can either remind them of what reality truly is to keep them going or it serves as a life reminder and sends them into a deeper depression or feeling depressed. Real world events such as the birth of a baby, an extension of the family through marriage, a promotion at work, an increase in pay, kids achieving good grades, individuals accomplishing personal goals, or a combination of any of the above are examples of what keeps people filled with hope, faith, and setting new goals and achieving them. Real world events bring joy, happiness, excitement, a sense of empowerment and self-gratification to people. People remain inspired to what the world has to offer but then there is the other side that people must deal with in their reality that is not so positive or happy-happy-joy-joy either.

Real world events present heartache, pain, grief, setback, trials, and tribulations, death, despair, loss of a job, uncertainty, fear, and depression that cause a low sense of self, a disconnect between fantasy

Dr. Tekemia Dorsey's (DTD) Transformational Leadership Models and reality for some, and oftentimes, forcing people to say things, do things and act in a manner that is unbecoming to their character and family values.

Real world events can either uplift or challenge one's state of mind. Real world events even if caused by a setback requires a strong comeback. One that is positive in nature and requires productivity of life. However for that to happen people must think critically through the situation, reach across the party lines to build their team of support and resources, understand the cultural diversity embodied in the scenario, but most importantly know who they are entering this journey, check self along the way, and evaluate their growth once it is over.

Real world events such as life struggles and challenges are meant for people to grow mind, body, soul, and spirit in every facet, role, responsibility, hat worn, relationships entered and exited along the way. For every situation we go through, we should come out of the other side of it, a new creature whether it be mind, body, soul, spirit or a combination of one or more of the above.

Real world events such as life struggles and challenges can be presented to people in different ways and impacting various stages of one's life. However, it is now what is presented to you in know that matters but it is, how you handle it. Women, for example as discussed earlier take on many roles, massive responsibilities, and usually overwhelmed themselves all in the matter of a day, week or month, with or without active children, a husband or extended family to care for.

Real world events such as becoming a mom for the first time, getting married, caring for an elderly parent, having a 2nd or 3rd child, being an active member in the community, serving as Team Mom of a child's organization event (sports, nonprofit organization), and even mentoring others are real things for women that cannot be altered or face anyway other than head on. Most women embrace, accept, and openly accept the journeys presented to them but not all women.

Some women do not want to be a mother or think they feel they want in the beginning to then realize, motherhood is not what they thought it would be or can now handle. Some women like the thought of being married, a wife, someone's partner only to find out that marriage is like a job but it takes time to learn what marriage is truly, to develop a formula for success, and to understand there is a HUGE difference between being single and being married. Once realized what is required to be married, in a marriage and to remain in a marriage, some women no longer remain interested in being marries.

Some women want to be viewed as philanthropic and are moved by the thought of volunteer work but it like marriage, being a wife, and having kids, too is work. It requires time, patience, good decision making, great communication, and the ability to know what she is already bringing to the table in terms of strengths and areas of improvement.

Dr. Tekemia Dorsey's (DTD) Transformational Leadership Models

When starting any new journey, new venture, new goals set, if a person truly embrace the strengths and areas of improvement within self, from the old, a new creature is born. When a person starts their day, from sun up when a person rises, to set down (when a person rests), a transformation from the old to the new should occur because when a person gains knowledge and applies it in terms of wisdom in each interaction, decision made, scenario presented and end result, a different person emerge. No every person understand or desire to know the transformation that happens on a daily basis but when they do, the probability of positive growth, development, and outcome I one's life remains endless.

When real world events become too much to bear, some people balance the reality of what is real with that of something higher in which they believe in, for the sake of this discussion, it is being identified as *Spiritual Guidance*. Real world events can either make or break the development of leaders however I believe that everyone is automatically born because of the Holy Spirit that dwells within.

Spiritual Guidance

Some people are motivated by the guidance of the Holy Spirit that lives within them. Instead of turning to the events of the world they intuitively listened to what the Holy Spirit says to them and encourages them to do in terms of movement, relationships, behaviors, etc.

Just like the events of the world, a person experience heartaches and pains, trials and tribulations, successes and failures however in addition to, or in opposition of real world events, people lean on the faith and comfort that the word of God to get them through tough times and cause for additional celebration during good times.

The guidance of one's faith and belief in a power higher than self is largely dependent of the individual and cannot be refuted in terms of impacts in one's life and affect in their behaviors and actions. However, who their higher power is whether its God, Allah, etc can be a topic of discussion.

In the application and training of Dr. Tekemia Dorsey's (DTD) Transformational Leadership Models, these two core pillars are what makes the difference in the models. One model is one of the secular nature (real world events) where real world events are used as part of the teachings and applications and whereas the other (spiritual guidance) is one of spiritual reflection and the principles enforced by the teachings of the bible are used in terms of delivery, re-enforcement and practical application of the training.

Whether it is real world events or spiritual guidance that motivates and guides a person through the journey he/she undergoes, the same remains is that there is or should be a transformation of the old to the new once the end result is reached, when a person allows growth to happen.

CORE PILLAR 6: *LEADERSHIP ATTRIBUTES*

Are leaders born or made? This discussion has been one that goes as far back as pre-historic dinosaurs, and depending on who you ask, can be answered one way or another. In my professional experience, leaders can be made and from my personal beliefs, leaders can be born. From my personal beliefs, everyone is born with a soul; which is in essence connected to the Holy Spirit. Through the guidance and facilitation from the Holy Spirit, individuals learn to know what is right and what is wrong in life. Individuals learn to know what is right and what is wrong through their parents, environment, culture, surroundings, role models, and society.

Those that are trusted to lead and guide these individuals are also filled with the Holy Spirit. When individuals are connected and remain connected with the higher being he/she believes in and stay connected with that higher being, then transformation begins from the inside out versus the outside in, that remains evident in their behaviors, actions, communications, choices made and the way people are impacted (Positive versus Negative, Selfish gain versus Selfless gain, Transformational versus Transactional).

Through the personal growth and development from a two-step process, leaders are born and not made. The two-step process encompasses the guidance and facilitation led by the Holy Spirit and

Dr. Tekemia Dorsey's (DTD) Transformational Leadership Models executed by individuals. All that is really needed in life is that of belief and execution of what we really are and that is a spiritual being living in a borrowed body which is known as the "flesh" therefore the POWER we need to be Leaders already exist inside each and every one, It simply needs to be tapped into needs to simply be tapped into, but if it were that simple, I would not have developed DTD's Transformational Leadership Models or feel the need to write this book.

"True Leadership Lies In the POWER of the HOLY SPIRIT"

Dr. Tekemia Dorsey

Through the training from Dr. Tekemia Dorsey's (DTD) Transformational Leadership Models, participants examine the actions of leaders and have an opportunity to speak to community leaders to further develop their concept of the characteristics and roles of transformational leaders. Additionally, participants explore, unveil, and accept the leadership attributes within each of them and apply those leadership attributes to their lives. Participants develop to develop a plan of action of their lives that allows for personal growth and development of their plans and desires of life (i.e. family, community, work, relationships, or career, etc).

Youth Leaders-In-Training

Dr. Dorsey's oldest son, Brandon, now 17 years old was a part of the original pilot study of students who engaged in and completed her leadership development, training and education certificate program using the spiritual leadership version of her transformational leadership model in a private Christian school in Baltimore County, MD when he was just in 3rd grade. From 3rd – 8th grades, Brandon engaged in the transformational leadership program, graduating from the program several times year after year.

Brandon has held and continue to hold leadership positions such as

1. Middle River Parks and Recreation Youth Football Coach Intern 2 Years
2. Hair Doctors Barbershop Intern – 8 years
3. Annual Adopt A Family Christmas Program – 11 years
4. National Literacy Mentorship Program – 5 years
5. Cristo Rey High School Intern – 3 years
6. Top Teens of America Vice President – 2 Years

Brandon now in his final year of high school, gave several speeches at a recent induction of youth for Top Teens of America Spring Induction Ceremony, his theme choice is reflective of his views and training endured over the years which has made him into the fine young scholar and leader he is today.

Dr. Dorsey developed the leadership development, training and educational curriculum and program originally to see if the

Dr. Tekemia Dorsey's (DTD) Transformational Leadership Models leadership concept could be taught on the elementary school level because a quality program did not exist. Dr. Dorsey taught the program and learned from its participants that graduated from the certificate program (K-12) within the first 5-7 years of the program demonstrated that if youth are taught core pillars of leadership training centered on their personal growth and development, then their future and that of our society and community remain more than hopeful and prosperous. Also as adults they will continue to have a positive impact on life.

Brandon C. Johnson,
Kenwood High School Senior
Age 17
Delivering GREAT LEADERS Speech
Top Teens of America Induction Ceremony
Spring, 2015

Great Leaders...

Awaken minds.

Bring people together.

Communicate effectively.

Dare to take calculated risks.

Enlighten and empower.

Foster collaboration.

Give you tools to succeed.

Help you do for yourself.

Invite and encourage questions.

Joyfully embrace diversity.

Keep an open mind.

Lead by example.

Motivate with respect.

Never give up on you.

Open doors to new worlds.

Put first things first.

Quest to make learning fun.

Recognize problems early.

Share roles and responsibilities.

Take time to explain things.

Unwrap talents and abilities.

Value everyone's input.

Welcome mistakes as part of learning.

Xceed expectations.

Yearn to connect, not correct.

Zest to make a difference.

Dr. Tekemia Dorsey's (DTD) Transformational Leadership Models

CORE PILLAR 7:
COMMUNICATION

Communication, if not handled properly can be a source of evil or the catalyst for a successful change. The sole reason why communication is important is because of the various levels and ways in which we can connect with each other. Communication is all about developing a connection with others and when connections are made, relationships are built. When relationships are built and nourished, success becomes remains imminent for all parties involved, regardless of the intellectual, number of degrees, socio economic status, racial, and ethnic, economic or religious affiliation.

Individuals learn early on that it is not about what you say to people but it is how you say it that matters. It is possible to offend someone in a nice way by using the right words at the wrong time. Just the tone of your voice is enough to change the message you are passing across

There are various ways to communicate and unlike the days of our forefathers, times have drastically changed, for the good from some but overall, not so much for society at large.

Our forefathers were forced to speak directly with one another face-to-face. Still with face-to-face communication the message can still be miss-interpreted by the tone, words used, and body language of the messenger and how those variables are received and interpreted by the

Dr. Tekemia Dorsey's (DTD) Transformational Leadership Models receiver make all the difference for relationships built and grow. As they say, the first impression makes a lasting impression.

Sender – Receive Message

Communication plays a large role in how you are perceived by others. The basic language for communication is English Language in the United States, however when communicating with others depending on their background, cultural, socio economic status, environment, or even ethnic affiliation, the basic English language can take on many levels when being interpreted. For example, the most common misinterpretation between

African Americans and Caucasians is the way in which the word "Negro" can be used and received.

Communication Barriers

For an African American to refer to another African American as a "Negra or Negro" it is not deemed as offensive, if a Caucasian was to refer to an African American as a Negro then an offence will be automatically be taken, Why is that? This is the case because of ethnic and cultural barriers that go back centuries. Rightfully so, words used and the meaning of that word depending on who says it and who is in receipt of it, makes a huge difference in successful or failed communication. Now that same word Negro in Spanish means Black which simply denotes a color and has not reference to race and cultural affiliations.

People communicate through language as well as dress, style choice. When most people see a person dressed in all black, regardless of race, cultural, socio economic status, etc. it is typically associated with death and mourning of a loss, however that is not always true and it often mistaken. People who are overweight and uncomfortable in their skin typically wear the color black because it makes them look slimmer which in turn make them feel better about self. The color black can also be viewed on teenagers as being gothic, weird, and even depressed which is not always true as

Dr. Tekemia Dorsey's (DTD) Transformational Leadership Models well. The color for teenagers is simply often just an expression or who they are such as the painting of their fingernails black and also wearing the color choice of black the majority of the time for various reasons.

Corporate women have been known to also use the color choice of black as their choice of nail polish for the work place for various reasons such as representation of colors of their favorite football team, an occasion of celebration, and so forth. Nevertheless, what we understand here is that communication portrayed through the intent of the sender and the manner in which one receives it, either helps in the success of communication or the detriment of failure.

When dealing with communication face-to-face, the manner in which the sender relates a message and the way the receiver receives the message will greatly impacts the success of relationships, While the face-to-face method continues to be the best method in which we communicate, it still have levels which needs to be considered and valued for success. We will explore that in the next book release and during training.

Times have changed drastically in terms of communication, largely in part to Y2K at the turn of the 21st century and ever since then, the manner in which we communicates have changed with the advent of the internet.

The Internet

The introduction of the Internet scared the majority of the world because it was so unknown however the launch of the Internet changed the way communication would forever be remembered as intimate, straightforward, clear cutting, and impactful.

The Internet took away the option of one's ability to communicate face-to-face. The Internet has created a situation whereby individuals are allowed to communicate without a real face and also for the receiver to interpret the message anyhow he/she feels. The Internet hindered rapport

Dr. Tekemia Dorsey's (DTD) Transformational Leadership Models and the building of relationships and opened up ways in which people could communicate secretly causing relationships to be destroyed on the one hand and relationships being built on the other hand.

Once companies begin to realize the power of the Internet in terms of efficiency, speed, quantity versus quality, additional ways to communicate using the Internet's technology quickly evolved. From pagers, to flip phone, to smart phones, to now watches, tablets, eye glasses, ear pieces, chips embedded in one's skin, etc. While all the advancement of technology through the Internet was deemed as beneficial to society, businesses, and the stock markets just to name a few, the backlash of it all remains the lack of effectively knowing how to communicate from a human to human point of view.

Individuals today, such as our youth, young adults and individuals seeking to climb the ladder of influence and leadership positions lack the proper training in the various ways in which to communicate with tiers of people within businesses, institutions of higher learning, as well as their very own peers. Unfortunately, a person cannot land a successful interview sending a text message to Human Resources for consideration. An individual cannot send a text message or tag a person on Instagram as a follow up to say "Thank You" for an interview. Communication on any levels should result with a "Win – Win" scenario for all parties involved, never one over the other.

Even with the most recent and often up to date technology, devices such as emoticons it is still not an effective method of communication and it devalues the relationships built and rapport between individuals. An individual in a job situation cannot communicate effectively using "smiley face emoticon" with his/her supervisor, superior, or even a secretary. It simply lacks professionalism and some people prefer not to even use technology other than good ole fashion face-to-face communication.

When exploring the topic of communication the discussion goes deeper than what is presented here, however in the training from the Dr. Tekemia Dorsey's (DTD) Transformational Leadership Models, participants examine the various ways in which messages are communicated—both verbal and nonverbal, and assess their effectiveness of communicating and interacting with various groups. The importance and role of communication in leadership is explored and participants have the opportunity to develop their own theories and strategies to improve communication within a group.

Core Pillar 8: *BEING TRANSFORMATIONAL*

Being transformational means the cause is greater than any one individual and while that sounds great in theory, it is even more important in execution. Individuals must be able to put aside ego, bias, prejudice, negativity, pass hurt, and even emotions that affect performance to create a positive environment that resonates well with others.

In any environment, individuals have the power to transform anything by simply being his/her self. When a person walks into a room, people will automatically know whether that person is approachable or not. Whether that person fits in a certain crowd, whether or not that person is warm and fuzzy or cold and distant. There is a saying that "First impressions are lasts forever" and these impressions can either have a positive or not so positive ripple impact.

When people know who they are; what they can offer, their strengths and areas of improvement; have a sense of balance and uncanny self-confidence, even on their bad days, they can either take the initiative to transform their societies or not. They have the ability to turn things upside down. They have the POWER within to simply change the atmosphere and culture in a room, an environment, and a person's mood by doing simple things right from the beginning.

Dr. Tekemia Dorsey's (DTD) Transformational Leadership Models

When a person is presented with a situation of adversity, she/he should be able to first remember who they are (their strengths, areas of weaknesses), should immediately begin to think critically through unveiling the hidden cues for success, developing a plan of action that includes building a team, understanding the cultural diversity embodied in the situation, reflecting on what motivates a person to think outside the box, identifying the leadership attributes possessed and those of persons around them, ensuring effective communication and follow up (being transformational in nature versus transactional). Working in the best interest of everyone versus a select few.

In training with Dr. Tekemia Dorsey's (DTD) Transformational Leadership Models, participants explore Johari's Windows again but in a different manner that allow them to identify various ways in which they can be agents of transformation in their communities and circles The Johari window – which represents self – looks like this:

Before

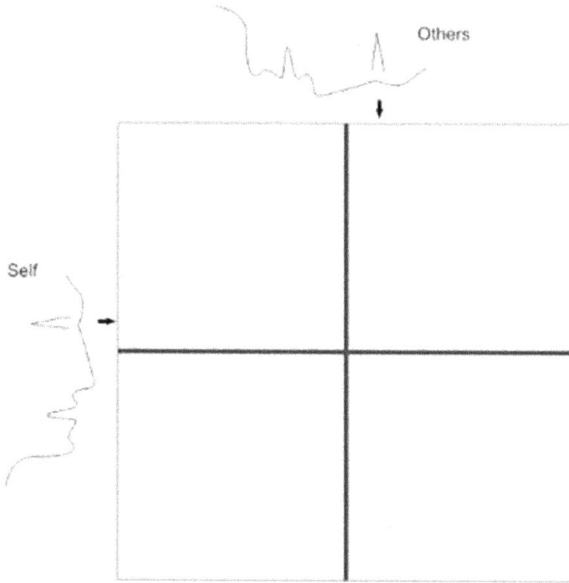

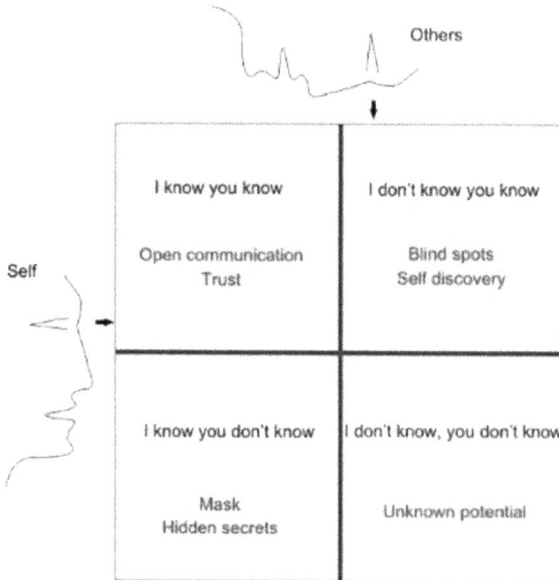

After

http://www.skills2lead.com/johari-window.html

Dr. Tekemia Dorsey's (DTD) Transformational Leadership Models Johari's Window is a tool used to help individuals become even more aware of self and to reaffirm self. This is a wonderful tool as a part of DTD's Transformational Leadership Model to assist people going from ordinary to extraordinary leaders.

I believe self-awareness is one of the greatest gifts we have in our tool box for success.

CORE PILLAR 9:

Who Am I – 360 Degrees of Evolution

A person that has evolved 360 degrees of evolution after going through each core pillar of this leadership model and have allowed growth to occur from the inside out. An individual goes from an ordinary individual to an extraordinary leader as they learn who they are and what they are truly capable of achieving. When applied to any scenario of life, due to a paradigm shift in thinking, outlook on life and self, participants are able to take the concepts learned and applied to any scenario in take, allowing for transformational leadership behaviors, actions, and outcomes.

Let's explore Dr. *Tekemia Dorsey's (DTD) Transformational Leadership Models* (360 Degrees of Evolution) applied to a scenario of someone wanting to become an entrepreneur.

Dr. Tekemia Dorsey's (DTD) Transformational Leadership Models

Dr. *Tekemia Dorsey's (DTD) Transformational Leadership Models* (360 Degrees of Evolution)

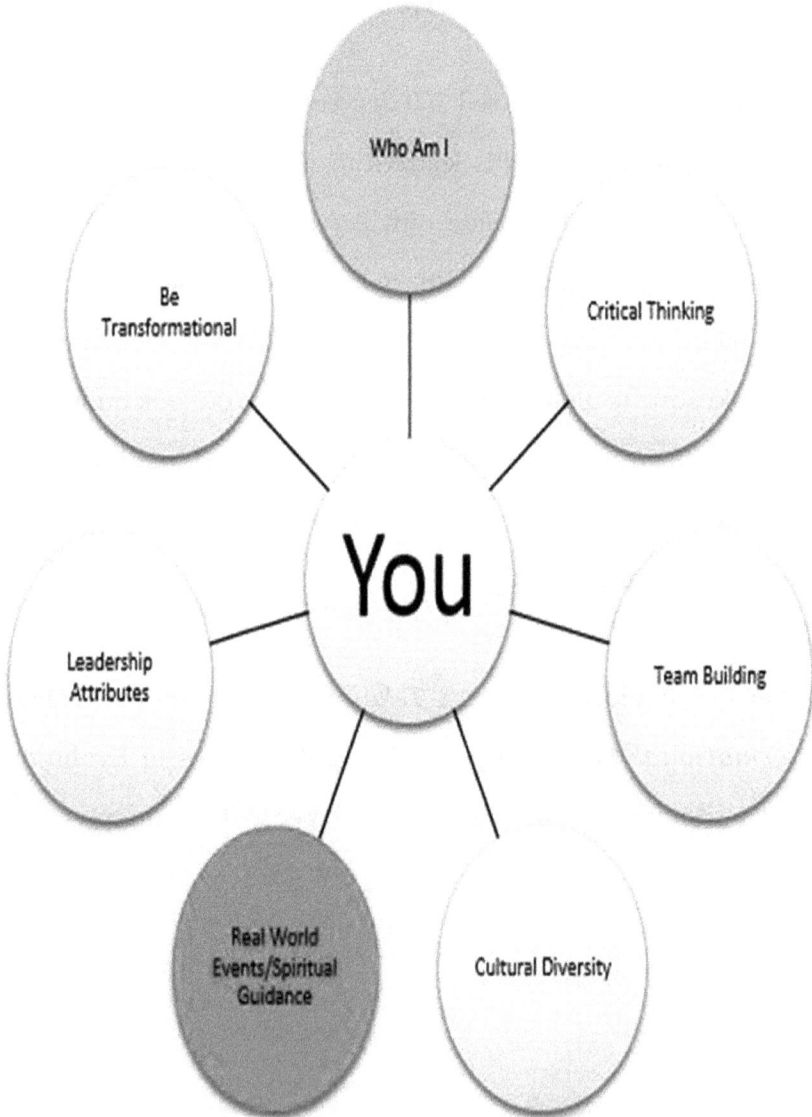

Become an Entrepreneur

To move past a business owner mentality into an entrepreneurial mentality, you must first explore, recognize and understand the concept of "_**Who AM I**_?" Understanding your strengths and weaknesses as a person and all the hats you wear in life, will help you determine how effective you will be as an individual, launching and continuing with your business successfully. Every business owner is not meant to be an entrepreneur.

To move past a business owner mentality to the entrepreneurial state-of-mind, you must _**critically think**_ through the process by developing an action plan for success, such as _**who you are**_, _**what you want to accomplish**_, and _**what resources will be needed to make your dream a reality**_. Moving a plan from thought into manifestation takes time, energy, and careful consideration. Plan your work and work your plan.

To move past a business-owner mentality into an entrepreneurial mentality, you must not only believe there is no "I" in team, but you must begin implementing the concept through _**team building**_ strategies. The challenge becomes not only exploring who you are, but knowing what you can contribute to a team in terms of leadership, what you can learn from those in teams and how to balance the two in business.

Dr. Tekemia Dorsey's (DTD) Transformational Leadership Models

To move past a business-owner mentality into an entrepreneurial state of mind, you must be able to identify and understand the ___cultural diversity___ of the world in business settings, business relationships, and the business culture of the organization. As an entrepreneur, you must understand the diversity that lies within each and every person you will come into contact with and never believe, think or treat others as if they are all lump together under one category. Knowing the uniqueness of culture and the impact that diversity has on business and within relationships will help your business go far. Each person on your team or part of your staff will bring similarities and differences to the table, but you as the leader will need to know how to balance the team successfully.

To move past a business-owner mentality into an entrepreneurial mentality, examine ___real world events___ that are occurring in life or seek ___spiritual guidance___ to ensure success. Events that happen in the world allow an entrepreneur that things will happen but it is not what happens that define you however it is how you handle it that make all the difference. Seeking spiritual guidance from someone or something in life you believe in, provides clarity and understanding on how to act, approach, and address concerns of interests that may arise. Every day in life, you will encounter expected and sometimes unexpected challenges but as an entrepreneur you must find the power within to overcome the adversity presented.

To move past the business-owner mentality to the entrepreneurial state of mind, you must identify the ___leadership attributes___ that you already possess and the ones that have yet to be identified. Leadership attributes that already exists within you were discovered at some point along your life/upbringing, or through positive characteristics from you identify as role models in your life. Identifying your leadership attributes, what you stand for such as trust, loyalty, respect, honesty, stability, etc) will allow your business to progress in a manner that is satisfactory to you and that you can help grow along the way. As its company's leader, the organization will take on your characteristics, beliefs, morals, and values that are either good or not so good. If you are unsure about the leadership attributes you possess, seek assistance from a Life Coach or one that specializes in leadership growth and development.

To move past the business owner mentality into an entrepreneurial mentality, you must first explore, embrace and to learn to execute effectively the art of **_communication_**. Communication is a major factor that will decide if a business will succeed or fail, which means it can catapult you forward in business or thrust you backwards as an entrepreneur and a leader. There are a multitude of ways to communicate such as verbal and non-verbal, the type of clothing used to express self, the behavior in which one acts and much more.

To move past a business-owner mentality into an entrepreneurial state-of-mind, you must learn to transform your environment by **_being transformational_** in your actions, words, and behaviors and through your relationships, culture and environments. The ultimate keys to

Dr. Tekemia Dorsey's (DTD) Transformational Leadership Models success are simple; understand the process and learning the process; the PROCESS OF SELF! You hold the key to transforming events, situations, failures, and successes of life.

A business owner is frequently short on time and does not have enough hours in a day to deal with everything needed to successfully operate a business, however, an entrepreneur finds a way to balance home, work, schools, family, relationships, along with personal and professional success.

Become A Corporate Executive

To become a corporate executive it takes a skill set beyond the ordinary employee or office worker. One has to be sharp in areas of life that are not part of the normal but the exception. To become a corporate executive you must first know what you are working with (strengths) and things you must improve upon (weaknesses). To become a corporate executive you must be able to step outside of your comfort zone to be successful. To be a corporate executive you cannot be humble or shallow when being criticize or receiving critique from others.

To be a corporate executive there are a few do's and don't's you should consider for success:

Don't's

1. *Do Not Procrastinate*
   a. Top Level Executives are not procrastinators in life but are truly meticulous in what they do and how it is done.

2. *Do Not Be Fearful*
   a. Top Level Executives are not fearful in taking risks or beyond the status quo to go around what they want.
   b. TLE's are not fearful of the unknown but allow it to motivate and inspire them to achieve their ultimate goals.

c. TLE's are not fearful of appearing vulnerable and not all knowing. In order to surround yourself with the best, you can not appear as the master of all things.

3. *Do Not Be Full of Doubt*

   a. Top Level Executives do not doubt the impact that can make when they stay in their respective lanes.

   b. Top Level Executive value themselves more than others because only they know what their strengths and areas of weaknesses are.

4. *Do Not Do Tomorrow What Needs To Be Done Today*

   a. Top Level Executives work long hours because they cannot afford to put off today that can be done tomorrow. This requires sacrifice and dedication to the position, to the cause, to your mission.

5. *Do Not Communicate Poorly*

   a. Top Level Executives speak succinctly to others and their bottom line language caters on the ROI (return on investment) syndrome. Do not communicate poorly your intentions or what you want others to know. To become a top level executive, you must become less wordy in discussion and more focus on the bottom line.

Do's

1. *Know Your Self*

   a. Top Level Executives don't allow their weaknesses outshine their strengths. Achieving any goal in life or not is largely based on knowing self, knowing your strengths and areas of improvement. However that is far from enough to get where you want to go. In knowing yourself you must know the "internal and external" and examine these two categories of life daily.

      i. Internal

         1. What is that one thing in life that brings you happiness and peace?

         2. How do you balance a Winning Schedule?

         3. At what time of the day, are you at your best?

         4. How do you balance life and work and family?

      ii. External

         1. What resources do you have in terms of people do you have to turn to for assistance?

         2. What do you do to ease stress related situations?

3. What foundational principles help to drive your motivation daily?

2. *Identify Successful Characteristics of a Leader*

a. Top Level Executives align themselves with greatness by surrounding self with those that have what they desire. To be the best, you must learn from the best and those better than him/her. As a result you are encouraged to identify leaders around you that you want to mimic. Learn to be charismatic and transformational versus transactional and authoritative. Be solution-oriented and task driven. Understand there is a solution for every problem presented.

3. *Work Smart and Not Hard*

a. To ascend to the level of top executives, you must understand the process outweighs the outcome. Learn the process of other success top executives. Learn the system and then allow the system to work for you. There are going to be pieces of the whole sum that are attractive to you and other pieces that are not. There may be pieces of 2-3 systems discovered that are appealing.....take those pieces and create your own but.... The point remains plan your work and work your plan. Do not attempt to go this journey without being equip with tools for success.

4. *Reach Across the Party Lines*

    a. To ascend to the level of top executive, you have to play with the big dogs. Meaning you are smart, wise, and good at something and while that's great, it is not good enough therefore you must surround yourself with people smarter, wiser, and better at their craft than you are. Don't be afraid to reach out to others who you necessarily do not agree with because that will be the very person you will learn the most from.

5. *Build Rapport and Strong Relations*

    a. To ascend to the level of top executive, learn how to effectively communicate and build relationships, not relationships based off of what you are going or attempt to get from it. On the contrary, a relationship that sustain the test of time and that you leave and re-enter on good terms is a relationship worth growing and keeping. Don't allow your inadequacies such as ego, bias, prejudice, misperception, or misunderstanding keep you from blessing others and being blessed.

To be a top level executive you have to know who you are, what you want, how you are going to get it, who is going to help you get it, what will you be required to learn in the process to grow, what motivations will be present to keep you focused and determined; what skills set are needed for success, how will you communicate along the way, how do you take your POWER and use it for good and finally

Dr. Tekemia Dorsey's (DTD) Transformational Leadership Models arrived at the final destination determined for you, TOP LEVEL EXECUTIVE.

The Balancing Act for Moms

Not everyone is meant to be a mom or blessed with kids. To be a Mom you must be extraordinary in nature and you must learn that as a Mom, you develop a selfish character about yourself. To be a Mom, you must consistently evaluate your past, present, and prepare for the future. As a mom, unfortunately, you do not have the leisurely of putting off tomorrow, as others, what is needed for today.

As a Mom, you must understand that the world overwhelms you daily, not necessarily by choice but definitely by force. As a Mom, you realize that there are only 24 hours in a day but your efforts from your love and care for another, exudes 48 hours of efforts in a 24 hour period.

As a Mom because you want to do so much for so many in the few hours of the day, you Mom, as a person get lost and have a hard time finding balance. As a Mom, in a 24 hour period, you may on average you an hour to yourself which is either because of a lunch break or the drive to and from home and even with that, most Mom's minds are racing at a 1000 miles a minute.

As a Mom, you must find time for yourself to balance harmony in your life and to revitalize your mind, body, soul, and spirits. Here are a few tips to balance your life as a Mom:

1. _**WHO Am I**_ – meaning identify what in life makes you happy (i.e. working out, sports, writing, drawing, alone time, meditation), etc.

2. *__Think Critically__* – Review your schedule, examine the best time of the day that provides you a time to enjoy the thing you identified in the Who Am I section. That time maybe in the early morning, late at night, or dead smack in the middle of the day.

3. *__Team Building__* – Now that you have a plan in place, you must know reach across the party lines to include people that can help you out, whether it is with your schedule or simply assisting you with time for yourself.

4. *__Cultural Diversity__* – Through this exploration stage, understand the dynamics of the diversity within your cultures that will have a positive or negative impact on your overall goal such as who you surround yourself with, the environment you leave your kids in that is different or similar to yours, etc. Doing so can either add to or extract from the lack of balance in one's life.

5. *__Real Life Events/Spiritual Guidance__* – As a Mom, what happens in the world scares us dearly as we are in the business of protecting our children and our loved ones. Even as Moms, we need an outlet, other than that other human insight and interaction for balance and
revitalization; therefore seek guidance from whatever power higher than self you believe in.

6. *Communication* – As a Mom, mastering the art of communication is a daily struggle especially when it comes to our kids and their success. As a result, learning to how to interact and build relationships and rapport is extremely important. It also provides a sense of peace when the end outcome is a Win Win for all.

7. *Leadership Traits:* As a Mom, you must know how to lead others around for success. For that to happen, you must examine what your leadership traits and one way is through reflection and journaling.

8. *Being Transformational*: As a Mom, when you are able to constantly examine yourself, how to make it fit in your life, identify your source of assistance, get to understand the various environments and cues around you, allow the events of the world to guide you but spirit to teach you and keep you humble/grounded, know what leadership traits your possess and how to lead others around you for success through communication, then you are able to be transformational in your own life.

9. *Who AM I – 360 Degrees of Evolution*: As a Mom, the prize in balancing one's life is not the outcome but the process endured along the way that allows for personal growth and development of the mind, body, soul and spirit. The person who starts the journey

Dr. Tekemia Dorsey's (DTD) Transformational Leadership Models of balancing from the beginning and advances through each stage of this transformational leadership model should not be the same; therefore allowing the person to go from ordinary person to an extraordinary leader from start to finish.

Become A Leader In Your Community

To become a leader in your community you must be mindful of what you stand for, what you believe in, what difference you want to make, and who you want to align yourself with. However before any of that happens, you must first explore the quality of your inner being. Being a leader in your community requires that you balance between your personal, your social and your professional arenas. While each these components differ in execution they, each are all very well connected to YOU.

Being a leader requires finesse, balance and support. It requires that you are have an understanding of the question WHO AM I? Only you can answer that question and how often you evaluate the question is a critical component of your success. Being a leader in the community requires that you have a great sense of time management, organization, and communication skills; understand, know and value diversity from others and in self; know your leadership traits possess; value and practice team building and above us, to be transformational in your position versus being transactional. If you are unable to say unequivocally I can do all these things (traits, etc), then keep on working on it to become a leader in your community.

The problem for those who are unable to answer the above with a resounding yes to most if not all things, is that people often take on positions and roles to believe the position/role held, will make him/her a leader. This could be far from the truth. To be a leader and an effective one, you must already possess certain traits and characteristics within you that will add value to the position.

To be a leader in your community, you must clearly understand the diversity of which you are dealing with. Diversity in education levels, socioeconomic status, cultural backgrounds and environments, communication barriers, and belief systems. As a leader in your community, you can be at the table with people of vast backgrounds, ethnicities, cultures, genders, etc who are supporting the same cause but are all filled with their own prejudices and bias. Your job as the leader in your group, at that table is to transform the environment and to bring everyone on one accord, despite their differences and similarities. You must be transformational in your efforts versus transactional. You, as the leader cannot appear bias, prejudice, show favoritism or one sided or you will lose support and respect quickly.

To be a leader in your community, you should build on your success through volunteer positions early on in your career. The greatest leaders were all once loyal and faithful followers. Even the most well-known and respected leaders today, remain in the position of student as well as teacher. Before becoming a leader in your community or while you are leading a charge in your community continue to volunteer your efforts in areas where you will continue to be in a position to growth and prosper.

To be a leader in your position, under the many languages spoken by others such as politics, inner-city, foreign language, cultural language, environment language, social cues, just to name a few. There are cultures inside of cultures hidden by more cultures in the world and your job is to become aware, acquainted, and married to these cultures to be successful as a leader in your community. Two of the greatest gifts you can possess as a leader in your community are being well-versed in cultural diversity and communication.

To be a leader in your community, you must be willing and open to be stretched outside of your normal comfort zone. To be a leader in your community, you must learn not to use people for selfish gain, to learn to be self-less in your actions. To be a leader in your community, you must remain optimistic and in pessimistic in nature and in execution. To be a leader in your community, you must critically thing through tough decision and draw conclusions on your own versus that of another.

Dr. Tekemia Dorsey's (DTD) Transformational Leadership Models

Become A Better Student

To become a better student, you must quickly realize what your interests are and are not. You must understand which subjects most hold your interest versus those that do not. You must understand that even those subjects you do not have the greatest interest in, has a greater interest in you. What does that mean you wonder? It simply means that all subjects are vital and important to your existence, success as a student and in becoming a productive member of society. WHO AM I?

Subjects such as reading, math, science, social studies, physical education, home economics, business, and wood shop, just to name a few all teach you ways to think, act, and problem solve through situations. Each of the subjects previously mentioned, you use in life daily in different ways and with different people. School provides universal principles of one's life that will only expand beyond graduation but the foundation is set while in school. CRITICAL THINKING!

To become a better student, you must learn to follow policy and procedures of life. You must understand that even policies and procedures you do not believe in or those you find irrelevant are quite relevant in and to your life. Much like the discussion on subjects above, policies and procedures are in place to protect you and to ensure you become successful in life. (REAL LIFE EVENTS)

Dr. Tekemia Dorsey's (DTD) Transformational Leadership Models

Policies and procedures were put in place by your forefathers as a guide for success because they had already experienced the trial and tribulations of downfalls and up rises, setbacks and comebacks, peaks and valleys and simply want you to be successful. The policies and procedures set in place are to ensure you go from where you are and reach where you are destined to go, in a path of less resistance. Life as you know it as a student is one to be desired because others are responsible for you until you turn the appropriate age to care for yourself. Once you reach that age of maturity, the policies and procedures of life, requires that you adhere to them appropriately or face the consequences of reality.

To be a better student, adhere to the teachings of your parents and adults around you. To be a better student, you must be an all-around better person. A student is merely a hat that you wear and a role in life you play but underneath that role, there remains "YOU" the person. There are people placed in your life to guide you, protect you and to facilitate your path but you do not have to listen to them and oftentimes, students do not listen to the adults in their lives without hesitation or resistance. (TEAM BUILDING)

To be a better student, do not fear help from others or asking for help for success. To be a better student, you must learn how to communicate with others around you when help is needed. There will be times in left when you are unsure of a problem in a subject, in life, in a situation, with people and knowledge from another is required. It does not make you less of a person to ask for assistance. It does not make you weak, it does not make you less of a man or less of a woman; it simply means you are smart enough to know you cannot do things alone.

Communication, like money **can be** the root of all evil and success. Communication unlike money _is_ the root of all evil and success. In life, there is no "I" in team and as the person leading the charge you must be know how to chat with people. You must learn how to talk "to people" and not "at people!" You must be learn to be able to communicate with people that wears suits, to people who wear jeans and a t-shirt, to people who hold positions higher than yours or you hold a position higher than them. When the dust settles and the smoke clears, the language spoken should be universal in nature and that makes you part of the norm and not the exception and that simply is the universal language of "RESPECT!" If you do not begin to understand how to communicate effectively with others, you career and the impact of your success as a student can be over even before it starts. The best measure in how you communicate with others, if first how you learn to communicate with your parents at home.

Excel In The Workplace

To excel in the workplace you must simply answer WHO AM I? Are you a lazy person? Are you a person that likes to be or need to be micromanaged all the time? Are you an independent or dependent thinker? Are you one that shows up on time, miss time from work, expect a raise but do have of the work required? Are you true to yourself and your own values? Are you know what skill set you have to offer of further need to develop? What do you know about yourself and are you honest about it?

If you are unsure who you are and what you have to offer, then you must critically think how to improve upon your foundation for success. For example, if you are often late to work and the expectation is to be there on time, then you must first learn to adhere to policy and procedures that govern the workplace to advance. If you demonstrate you are a misfit (someone that cannot fit the norm like others) that cannot follow the basic requirements for success, then excelling in the workplace may not happen or as quickly as one would like or even at all.

To excel in the workplace but you remain unsure of who you are, you must seek assistance from others for help. You must be willing to release ego and pride to build a team of support for your success. While Rome wasn't built overnight, feedback from a team of peers for success can. This would require for you to step outside of your comfort zone

Dr. Tekemia Dorsey's (DTD) Transformational Leadership Models and to align yourself with those who can provide quality feedback that is honest and

constructive in nature however.......you must be ready for the feedback good, back, or indifferent. Peers are always helpful in providing best practices with others, it is just a matter of them being asked the question.

To excel in the workplace, you must understand the cultural diversity that exists in your environment. Once you identified the cultural barriers that exist you have to position yourself to either one side (left vs right) or simply remain neutral. In organizational settings you may experience "clicks" that exist, for or against administration, for or against policy and procedures, for or against change management and so forth. Clicks are simply people that appear to have something in common and hence stick together along as they share the same issues, etc. Positioning yourself for a Winning outcome is important and all it takes is that you get to know the environment in which you work. Great thing is that it will not take long to figure it out or it figure you out.

To excel in the workplace, you must know the leadership qualities you possess and those you quickly must acquire to be successful. Every person has a certain skill set and ability that sets them apart from others. It is not only enough to know what your skill sets are and those that must be acquired but you must understand how to use them to your advantage to make you an asset to your organization and ultimately yourself.

To excel in the workplace, you must know how to communicate on all levels, to varying audiences, in a professional and non-threatening manner. To excel in the workplace, you should not speak to your boss as you would your co-worker because their positions and roles are different. To excel in the workplace, an email you send to someone you are dating that is a co-worker should be vastly different than sending one to a co-worker that you are not dating. To excel in the workplace, the tone used for a person who job is in the IT department is going to be different than a person who responsibility is customer relations. To excel in the workplace, you must know how to be respectful when communicating versus disrespect regardless of your targeted audience.

To excel in the workplace, you must be able to being transformational in your efforts. There is two sides to this concept (1) as it relates to self and (2) as it relates to the organization. Being transformational in an environment or setting is simply exerting the POWER you possess within outwardly for others to gravitate towards accept and embrace. Your passion, your purpose, your finesse, your positive energy, and even your charisma is what people gravitate to in life and especially in the workplace. No one wants to work with someone that is a 24/7 Grumpster. The POWER you possess when exerted resonates in behavior, interactions, decision making, and even

Dr. Tekemia Dorsey's (DTD) Transformational Leadership Models communications and transforms others around you through connections made. Being transformational within the organization requires that you act more on behalf of those you are responsible for, as a leader than yourself. In other words, don't be selfish but self-less. Make decisions that will benefit the cause versus any one individual. Being transformational in an organization especially in a leadership position can be tough but it does not have to be, if you remain true to yourself and are not swayed by politics.

To excel in the workplace, one must view the environment as one where real world events occur daily. What happens at work is happening all around the world and should be handled with care. When you view a person being fired for what appears to be an unjust cause that is real. When you hear of a person smoking illegal substance on an organization's property that is real. When a person is having a bad day at home and bring those issues to work that is real. When a person is place in a position of leadership but may not have earned it that is real. Many people in life, not all, view their workplace as they do their lives. Not many can separate and actually do separate the two but they should. When this happens, people viewing their workplace as their lives, their behaviors, values, actions and decision making begin to overlap and the potential for conflict arises. What can you learn from people in your workplace to excel further? You can learn first and foremost, to be true to yourself and to act, behave and treat others accordingly as you would want to be treated.

FROM ORDINARY TO EXTRAORDINARY

Someone asked me the question "360 degrees of evolution - wouldn't that put you on the same spot?" My answer is "ABSOLUTELY…. YES, what happens is that the person exits as a new creature after having gone through the evolutionary process that warrants the change in between" they end right back on the same spot but with a different outlook of self.

Now let's drive deeper into the nine core pillars chosen for these transformational leadership models and further understand why they are so significant in the development of you are a leader.

Dr. Tekemia Dorsey's (DTD) Transformational Leadership Models

Each module is an independent pillar of its own but are also dependent on one another for success as a leader.

The core pillars my DTD's Transformational Leadership Models have been discussed in this book individually. Through stories and real life scenarios, the model itself has been shared in practical application in how they work together to have ordinary people transformed into extraordinary leaders by experiencing the *360 Degrees of Evolution.*

The DTD's Transformational Leadership Models are universal across industries and disciplines respectively and is applicable to individuals from individuals such as youth, to CEO's of Corporation.

This book should be used interchangeably in academic settings and business cultures and environments. The contents of this book can be used as part of curriculum for youth in primary grades and on secondary levels, for those individuals going through workforce development programs, for students who are pursuing advanced degrees, for individuals looking to start a business, enhance their business, or to climb that ladder of success in positions within their corporate settings.

The DTD's Transformational Leadership Models core pillars are ones that focus on personal growth and development of a person and their behaviors. The content of the book can be used as part of any structural program, training or activity that focuses on improvement of self, soft skills development and as such but not limited to professional development, leadership training, personal growth and development.

Dr. Tekemia Dorsey's (DTD) Transformational Leadership Models are designed to take ordinary people and transform them to extraordinary leaders through 360 degrees of evolution through a focus on nine core pillars. Let's recap the component of each pillar:

Conceptual Component Summaries

1. *Who Am I?*—The key to being an effective leader is to have a true understanding of who you are as an individual and the roles that you play in your life circles. Participants begin to make the connections between their individual identities and the roles they play in their lives.

2. *Critical Thinking*—In order to develop a true understanding and application of the key components and characteristics of transformational leadership, participants explore the ways that they process and learn information in a variety of situations to develop a fundamental understanding of the ways in which they process

   information to make decisions as transformational leaders. Through an examination of Gardner's theory of Multiple Intelligences and Johari's Windows, participants have the opportunity to create their own strategic learning plan as the precursor to developing strategic plans for groups/teams that they may be leading through their roles as transformational leaders.

3. *Team Building*—A hallmark of transformational leaders is their ability to bring together individuals within a group to work together, collaborate effectively and ultimately grow into

Dr. Tekemia Dorsey's (DTD) Transformational Leadership Models

becoming leaders themselves—taking direct responsibility for the outcomes of their actions. Participants examine the dynamics of group interaction and the importance of team building in the transformational leadership process.

4. *Cultural Diversity*—A good transformational leader must consider the backgrounds and cultural footprints of their team in order to make sound decisions. As part of the unit, participants explore the effect that cultural norms, beliefs and ways of thinking affect group dynamics and impact leadership decisions across a variety of situations.

5. *Real World Events*—Participants examine real world events and critically assess the role of leaders in each situation. This examination of real-world application of leadership theory allows participants to further develop their understanding of the concepts presented.

6. *Leadership Attributes*—Participants examine the actions of leaders and have an opportunity to speak to community leaders to further develop their concept of the characteristics and roles of transformational leaders.

7. *Communication*—Participants examine the various ways in which messages are communicated—both verbal and nonverbal, and assesses their ability to communicate and interact effectively with various groups. The importance and role of communication in leadership is explored and participants have the opportunity to

develop their own theories and strategies to improve communication within a group.

8. *Being Transformational*—This component provides participants with a way of putting the theory of Johari's Windows into practice and identify various ways in which they can be transformational leaders in their communities.

9. *Who Am I*—This component provides participants with an opportunity to express who they are as transformational leaders, after have gone through each of the core pillars through this transformational leadership model.

You can surmise from the conceptual summaries of the core pillars, numbers 1 & 9 are both the same and that is not by mistake but rather by divine intervention.

Individuals begin the process of transformational leadership but exits the process as a new creature of habit and having experience 360 Degrees of Evolution. The 360 Degrees of Evolution occurs, when and only when, the individual is honest with self by identifying his/her strengths, areas of weaknesses and remains optimistic to change from stage one of the leadership model.

The nine core pillars of these transformational leadership models are not meant to be a means to an end, but a stepping stone or a continuation of self-exploration with a focus of leadership that leads to positive change and outcomes in one's life. Any of the core pillars can be made interchangeable with other pillars, models or programs to add a stronger value to the objective and goal at hand.

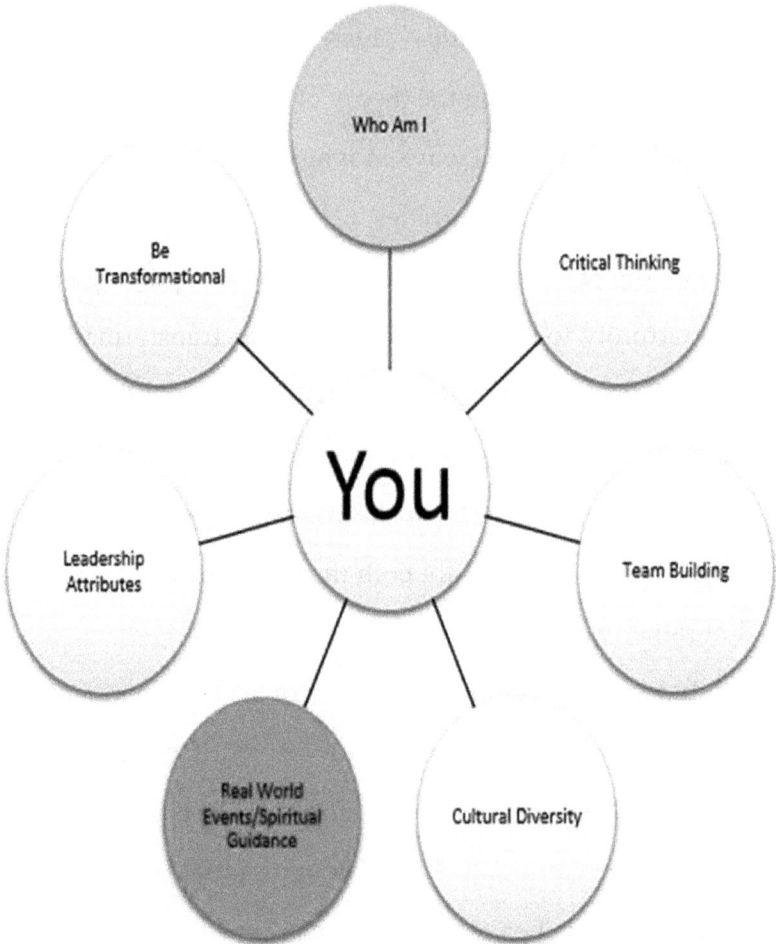

Dr. Tekemia Dorsey's (DTD)

Transformational Leadership Models

360 Degrees of Evolution

www.ingramcontent.com/pod-product-compliance
Lightning Source LLC
Chambersburg PA
CBHW070408200326
41518CB00011B/2112